The Mysterious Key to the New Testar
Copyright 2018 King

ALL RIGHTS RESERVED. No part of this ݀
system, or transmitted in any form or by any means - electronic, mechanical, photocopy, recording, or otherwise - without the written permission of the publisher, except in the case of brief quotations embodies in critical reviews and certain other non-commercial uses permitted by copyright law. For permission requests, write to the author via the website below:
www.churchinoneaccord.org

Special discounts are available on quantity purchases by corporations, associations, and other orders by US trade bookstores and wholesales-for details, contact the author via the website above.

All biblical quotations and language are taken from printed versions of the Bible, NKJV, NIV, Amplified, NASB.

NKJV - The Holy Bible, New King James Version Copyright © 1982 by Thomas Nelson, Inc. The New King James Bible, New Testament Copyright © 1979 by Thomas Nelson, Inc. The New King James Bible, Old Testament Copyright © 1980 by Thomas Nelson, Inc. Nelson, Thomas. Holy Bible, New King James Version (NKJV) . Thomas Nelson. Kindle Edition.

NASB - New American Standard Bible-NASB 1995 (Includes Translators' Notes) Copyright © 1960, 1962, 1963, 1968, 1971, 1972, 1973, 1975, 1977, 1995 by The Lockman Foundation, A Corporation Not for Profit, La Habra, California.
All Rights Reserved (1)

The Lockman Foundation. New American Standard Bible-NASB 1995 (Includes Translators' Notes) (Kindle Locations 1410-1412). The Lockman Foundation. Kindle Edition.
NIV - The Bible text used in this edition of the Life Application Study Bible is the Holy Bible, New International Version.® Life Application Study Bible copyright © 1988, 1989, 1990, 1991, 1993, 1996, 2004, 2005 by Tyndale House Publishers, Inc., Carol Stream, IL 60188. All rights reserved.

Tyndale. Life Application Study Bible NIV (Kindle Locations 11-14). Tyndale House Publishers, Inc.. Kindle Edition.

Amplified Bible - The Lockman Foundation - Copyright 1954, 1948, 1962, 1964, 1965, 1987 by The Lockman Foundation - All right reserved.

First Edition, 2018
ISBN: 978-1-970062-03-8
Publisher: Kingdom Mysteries Publishing
817 W Park Row, Arlington, TX 76013
Printed in the United States of America

Contents

1 - The Old Man

Origin and Nature	2
The Nature of the Old Self	10
God's Solution For The Old Self	13

2 - The New Man

A creative act of God	20
The New Man Manufactured	23
How To Develop The New Man	26
God's Agenda for the New Self	34

3 - The War of Natures

Romans 5:12-8:39	42
Romans 6	46
Freedom To Obey God's Spirit	51
Struggle With Sin And Evil	55
The Victorious Life in the Spirit	58

The Mysterious Key to the New Testament:
Secrets of the Old Man and New Man

Bruce Hines

1 - The Old Man
Origin and Nature

I would like to start this chapter off by making a powerful statement about two persons in the New Testament that have a position of unique importance. This statement is the key to coming to the correct understanding, I could even say, a total revelation of the New Testament. The truth is that we can never properly comprehend the message of the New Testament until we really come to the revelation of these two persons. It is of both theological and supernatural importance that we completely understand their origins, natures, and destinies. This will help us correctly divide the word of truth with the possibility of maturity if factually administered. It will also help us understand ourselves as we proceed through the sanctification process. Paul the Apostle never gives them a name, but gives them a title. Are you ready for it? They are the old man and the new man. Some entitle them as the old self and the new self. I will be using both titles in this chapter. Again, the truth is, we can never really understand the message of the New Testament until we come to the true reality of these two persons—the old self and the new self. I would also say that most in the body of Christ have not understood these two persons, and in so doing they fail to live a victorious life in Christ Jesus. So let us look at Ephesians 4:20-24:

But you did not learn Christ in this way! If in fact you have [really] heard Him and have been taught by Him, just as truth is in Jesus [revealed in His life and personified in Him], that, regarding your previous way of life, you put off your old self [com-

pletely discard your former nature], which is being corrupted through deceitful desires, and be continually renewed in the spirit of your mind [having a fresh, untarnished mental and spiritual attitude], and put on the new self [the regenerated and renewed nature], created in God's image, [godlike] in the righteousness and holiness of the truth [living in a way that expresses to God your gratitude for your salvation]. Ephesians 4:20-24 AMPB

Paul makes a clear distinction between both natures within the believer. He points out that it is the choice of the individual to which nature, the old self or the new self, one would yield too. In verse 17, Paul states that we should no longer walk as the Gentiles. The implication is that we as believers could possibly live as Gentiles or unbelievers even though we are already Christian. The word "Walk" means to make one's way or progress. It refers to the choice in how someone would regulate one's life; the decisions one would make as opportunities became apparent. Paul is saying, as we live life, a certain behavior would come forward that could possibly bring about continued actions that would resemble that of an unbeliever. In verse 17 Paul is clearly talking about the unbeliever, but by the time he gets down to verse 22, Paul reveals his point. He is saying, the believer has a nature that would show itself as deceitful, lustful, corrupted, just as the unbeliever. This old self, as Paul names, would definitely try to influence the believer's conduct while alive in the body during this evil age.

Paul is writing to committed Christians and instructing them to no longer live as ungodly people do. He says, and even insists, that Christians are to abandon all parts of their former life and live for the glory of Christ Jesus. And, given that Paul sees himself as with or in Christ, hence, he is instructing for Christ Himself. The Bible is directing us to no longer order or have arranged our behavior as the unbelievers do from their futile mindset. For the believer to have parts of their mind worldly, is to have a mindset that is useless or empty. This is why so many people, believers and non-believers, experience a lifestyle that brings no satisfaction, because their minds are set on the wrong things and emptiness is all they have. Paul tells the Ephesians that there is a good possibility that they have not heard the truth and or understood their position in Jesus. This is a fact today! Many Christians are so deceived about their position in Christ and their condition according to the old man. Believers quickly want to say, their old man was crucified in Christ but moments later, they go out and sin. Believers also want to say that on the cross Jesus became a curse for us, but moments later will go and sin, and thereby revealing the curse in their members. Positionally, our old self was crucified on Jesus' cross in Christ, but what Paul is revealing is the fulfillment of that work on the cross will come at the end of this evil age. Until the return of Christ, Christians will have two natures! This is why Paul says to lay aside or to put away, put off our old self. To cease doing what is customary from the old life. We are to remove everything that brings corruption through sin. This is a choice! We are to stop yielding to that which Jesus killed on the cross—the sin nature.

When we read our scripture again, we see the old self and the new self. As Christians, we are instructed to take specific actions in regard to these two selves. We are to put off the old self and put on the new self. I like to think of it as getting dressed. It takes time and thought to what I'm going to wear before getting dressed. The same with getting undressed, it takes time to undress and where I'm putting the dirty clothes. Theology calls this sanctification. Like getting dressed and undressed, it takes time and knowledge to properly go through the sanctification process. If we are going to do this, we must understand what is involved. So first, identification of the old self and the new self is a must, otherwise, how do we know if we are doing what scripture commands, the putting off or the putting on the two selves respectively? What I'm saying is, accurate scriptural knowledge is essential to the success of this process.

Let us now talk about the origin and nature of the old self. This is a reality that quite a few believers refuse to believe, yet it affects their decision making, the words they speak, and their actions in everyday life. Paul reveals in verse 22 of Ephesians 4, three key thoughts. Paul says the old man is corrupt, it lusts, and is deceitful. What is the meaning of deceit? It means to cheat, deceive, and beguile. From the old self we act dishonestly and treat ourselves and others unfairly. The old self likes to take advantage of others and situations in order to benefit itself. The old self wants to defraud the new self of everything that has been given in Christ Jesus. To defraud, Vine's defines it as to be robbed through the corrupt condition of the mind. The informal meaning of cheating is to be sexually unfaithful. This is an act or product of the old self, to be sexually immoral. Paul tells the Thessalonians in 2 Thessalonians 2:10 that all deceit reveals itself through unrighteousness. This is why nothing good comes from the old man. The old man is deceitful and in so being, all manner of unscrupulous words and deeds come forth. From deception sin came forth!

Paul says in Romans 16:18, that believers can be seduced by false teachers and their teachings. This happens as these smooth talkers speak what people want to hear and not the truth. This teaching is like flattery and deceives the minds of naive people. Anyone who does not believe Paul, Peter, and James has fallen from truth. The old self is programmed from the lie and, through hollow and deceptive doctrine, it leads believers into captivity. Peter says these false teachers and doctrines, mouth emptiness (deceit) through boastful words that are appealing to the lustful desires of the old self, they entice people to live in error (2 Peter 2:18). New Testament writers continue to teach to be watchful of being led astray by the sinful desires of the old man. The old man then is a seductive force that works against God's saving grace and the inheritance believers are to have in this age and the age to come. James, like Paul, speaks of the deceitful desires of the old self by using imagery of sexual seduction to show how our desires gradually, in subtle ways, bring about harmful effects. These insidious desires of the old self pull us in the wrong direction. James 1:14-15 of the NIV says, "Each one is tempted when, by his own evil desire, he is dragged away and enticed. Then, after desire has conceived, it gives birth to sin; and sin, when it is full-grown, gives birth to death." James spells it out for believers, the twelve tribes or the Christian Jews he was writing to.

The origin of the old self is deception! The old self is the product of deceit or deception. Deception's origin is in Satan.

The old self is the result of heeding Satan's lie. This is why mankind is so responsive to lies, it pulls its strength from the old self.

In reading Ephesians, a great deal of the imagery is about the Church. We could say, the imagery of the old self and new self is much like the archetypal (certain kind of person) pattern of the old Adam and the new Adam or the old humanity and the new humanity. One nature takes its pattern after deceit, lusts, and corruption, the other after truth, righteousness, and holiness.

James, Peter, and John identify the old man with the world or people at enmity with God, that is, those who are in opposition to God's will and purpose. We must come into an understanding that it is the fruit of the Spirit of God that produces God's work in us. The word "work" in Galatians 5:19 means toil as an effort and occupation. It has the implication of an act or deeds, meaning to labor in a business. In the gospel of Mark 1:24, the demon says, "what business do we have with each other, Jesus of Nazareth?" The conversation was about a place of employment. The demons job was to bring about the works of the flesh for entry. If we continue to be undisciplined and self-indulgent, the Holy Spirit will not aid in the sanctification process and doors of entry open to evil. Our carnal nature is similar to an enemy living inside us. It wants what it wants, and Paul says the only way for the old self not to deceive us is to crucify it.

Paul was not an immature Christian when he wrote Romans 7. Paul acknowledges that the old self will be with him during his life in this evil age. He says that the old self has nothing good within its nature. We cannot expect any good to come out of it. Even if we were to crucify the old man completely, it would still be with us, just not alive. This truth is seen in death. Paul said, when the law of God came, he died. The law of God revealed the work of the old man. As stated before, the product of the old self is deception, and everything that deceives has its origin in Satan. Adam and Eve found this to be true. Genesis 3:1 uses the word cunning or crafty, speaking of the serpent, Satan. The primary root in the Hebrew is to defraud through acts of treachery. Treachery is an act of betrayal of trust. It is a deceptive action within a nature. Satan, the leader of the fallen angels, got Adam and Eve to betray their trust of faith in God for false information or the lie. The Hebrew word also defines it as to deceive. The nature of Satan was to conspire against God and he fell for doing it. Adam and Eve listened to Satan, and in so doing, they conspired within. The result was to be beguiled or to be charmed, that is, to be enticed or lured to obey Satan. Once they did, they came under a new government and fatherhood. Mankind's father would now be Satan and the government would be sin.

There is another translation of the Hebrew word cunning, it is wiles. We are warned by Paul in Ephesians 6:11 that we must watch out for the devil's schemes or wiles. Notice, the armor of God is for the fallen angels and not the demons. Satan is a metaphor for the fallen. Authority in Christ Jesus is to handle the demonic realm, which is in the earth. From the beginning, creation has had its origin in God's Word, God said and it came to be. In Genesis 2:17 God said, you are free to eat from any tree in the garden, but you must not eat from the tree of the knowledge of good and evil, [now notice this] when [a timing word] you eat of it you will surely die[curse for disobedience]. Now, in Genesis 3:4, Satan said you will not surely die. The temptation was to ignore God's warning, and to disobey what God had told them. The lie was the direct negation or contradiction of what God had said. The belief and act of the direct lie gave birth to the old self.

From the start of this Chapter, I have been driving at one main point, the primary weapon of Satan and the fallen angels against the human race is deception. In Revelation 12:9 the Bible says, Satan and his angels lead the whole world astray. The word astray means to deceive, to lead away from the right way or truth. The fallen, this includes Satan, seduce the world and cause humanity to wander away from the truth. The Bible pictures Satan and the fallen angels as snakes. A snake will never be straight, but crooked! So the product of the lie is as crooked as the snake itself. This is the old self, crooked like Satan. Jesus says that Satan has been lying from the beginning. The lie fathered the old self, just as truth (Jesus) fathered the new self.

Deception sets in motion a process of degeneration. Deception produces lust, and lust is perverted rebellious desires. They are desires that are opposite in nature to the will of God. They are also opposed to the wellbeing of the one who entertains and acts on those lusts. Lust also has a fruit—sin—and sin produces death.

The Nature of the Old Self

There is a nature produced by deception and lust. The key word which describes it is corrupt. The nature of the old self is corrupt. This means it is also corruptible. This speaks of a moral decay going through a process for final ruin. The old nature, which is with us until we go to heaven or Jesus comes back, desires to go through a series of actions or steps to be taken in order to achieve a particular end—death. The old self wants to seem natural, causing an involuntary series of changes that bring about sin.

The old self is the offspring of Satan. This reality is found in Genesis 3:15 (AMP),

"And I will put enmity (open hostility) Between you and the woman, And between your seed (offspring) and her Seed; He shall [fatally] bruise your head, And you shall [only] bruise His heel."

The Lord spoke to the serpent concerning his seed. Because the old self is the offspring or the seed of Satan, it reproduces the nature of Satan. This means the old self has the basic or the inherent features of sin, thereby, demonstrating satanic characteristics. Jesus says in John 8:44, to the religious leaders of His day, "you belong to your father, the devil." We could say then, the devil is a father to the children of disobedience. Where disobedience is in our lives, there is the satanic principal at work. Let me say it this way, it is a person, a demonic spirit or fallen angel, causing us to live and act as their agent or representative. Simply put, the nature of the spirit being is reproduced in those who are disobedient. This is how a Christian can have a demon.

We can easily discern if this is the case by the word rebellion. When we act in disobedience to the Word of God or resist the move of the Holy Spirit, it is revealed that within any person, a demonic spirit is at work. The behavior of the old nature is rebellious in its nature. The function of the old self is to lead the believer away from holiness. Instead of the believer seeking purity, the old man's desire is to defile. When that happens, open doors for evil spirits take place for entry. The old man is ceremonially unholy to God. The flesh of mankind has taken on the nature of Satan and it is defiled. One of the definitions is to dye with another color or the staining of a glass. The old self has been polluted through moral and physical defilement, it has been blemished. Isaiah 53:6 (AMP) says,

All of us like sheep have gone astray, We have turned, each one, to his own way; But the Lord has caused the wickedness of us all [our sin, our injustice, our wrongdoing] To fall on Him [instead of us].

The old man caused us to wander from a proper belief or a course of action and to be lead astray or error through the seduction of sin. The mark of the old man in its behavior is to turn to its own way. Isaiah says that the old self turns its back on God, seeks its own will, its pleasure, and satisfaction without reference to God. It takes no action or suggestions in view of God. This is described in greater detail in Ephesians 2:1-3 (NKJV),

And you He made alive, who were dead in trespasses and sins, in which you once walked according to the course of this world, according to the prince of the power of the air, the spirit who now works in the sons of disobedience, among whom also we all once conducted ourselves in the lusts of our flesh, fulfilling the desires of the flesh and of the mind, and were by nature children of wrath, just as the others.

Colossians 2:13 says we were dead in our transgressions and the uncircumcision of our flesh or in 1:21, alienated and hostile in mind, engaged in evil deeds. King David said in Psalm 51:5, he was brought forth in iniquity, and in sin his mother conceived him. We see in Ephesians that the product of the lie is the sons of disobedience. Paul says the old nature wants to live according to the course of this world, that is, the way it operates through its beliefs. This passage of Scripture is a description of those who still have the old self. Paul says, Satan and the fallen angels are able to work in them, believer or non-believer, because of disobedience. Thus, the key here is that Satan is able to work in them through rebellion. Paul goes on to say, we all once conducted ourselves in the lusts of our flesh. Notice the free will to obey these lusts. These lusts are in reference to those evil desires which are ready to express themselves in bodily activities. They are seated in the emotions of the soul and or the natural tendencies toward evil things. We could say, they are passions that exist in the soul and emotions that desire to express themselves in activities. Notice again how Paul says that the old man wants to fulfill the desires or lusts of the flesh and of the mind. The satanic principle works through the unrenewed mind, an established stronghold in our emotions, working or producing through sinful acts. Remember we said the satanic principle is a foundation and system of beliefs that cause behavior by a chain of reasoning, which are all based on lies. We all notice people with beliefs, behavior, and attitudes that line up with the course of this evil age. The person's behavior is manifest in a number of applications that vary according to its yielding to the old man who has been fathered by Satan. By nature, we are sons of disobedience and disobedience always bring about God's wrath. Here is Paul's meaning throughout his epistles to the Church, there is a rebel living inside each one of us believers. Recapping, Satan's deception produces lust, lust produces sin, sin produces death. The nature of the old self produced in this way has two distinctive marks: first of all, it is corrupt spiritually, morally, physically; and secondly, it is a rebel.

God's Solution For The Old Self

If we are to really understand the New Testament, the mystery of the old self and new self is of vital importance. So much doctrinal error has come forth from this mystery. Bible mysteries are things which were hidden in the past, but now are to be brought out in the light. The old self is a problem that confronts every one of us. It is a theological understanding that presents itself to all humanity. It cannot be explained away or covered by some error of interpretation or a blanket scripture. When we misdiagnose ourselves through scriptural error, we are brought into the realm of arguments or face to face hostility with others and even ourselves. The entire human race, as long as we live in this evil age, is plagued with the old self. Why? We in the flesh have all descended from Adam. This is the disease that has come to humanity—sin.

For us to understand God's solution, we must rule out certain methods that are not scriptural but seem to be ingrained deep within the Church. Churches generally promote and advocate self-realization, which is a teaching on the fulfillment of someone's potential outside of the leadings and promptings of the Holy Spirit for sanctification; and telling believers to do-it-yourself through character and stating from a position in Scripture; as well as leaving the believer to act in the flesh on falsely fulfilling their own righteousness. These lead to what I call self-fulfillment and the believer trying to achieve it by striving for scriptural hopes and ambitions without the empowering work of the Holy Spirit. And here comes another issue in the Church—self-expression. Everyone has their own thoughts and feelings, which depend on their own desires, scriptural or not. Let me give you an example. The Bible clearly states that we shall not tattoo, yet believers have their own individual self-expression. Have you noticed the word "self?" Christians will say, well that is old covenant, yet Paul the Apostles says, I would not have known what sin was unless the law revealed it. Sin has its origin in the satanic nature, this is Bible doctrine 101. Self-expression can be stated as one who works out their own salvation. All these things give freedom to the old self which is a rebel in God's view. All solutions which have their foundation in self are giving free reign to a rebellious nature.

We also see within the Church a system of law, that is, believers turning to the law to deal with the old self. Here is one that may sting, the works of the Holy Spirit were for the Apostles and they passed away after the early Church was founded. This belief is described in one word—legalism. Israel's failure is proof that living by a set of laws does not achieve God's desired end. Paul in Romans 7 states that the law is holy, righteous, and good. So there is nothing wrong with law, but law cannot change the rebel. The law actually disapproves of the rebel and condemns him to death. This is why we don't tattoo. Why did I pick tattooing as my example? Because it brings out those self-expressions, self-realizations, and self-fulfillments. Religion does not change the rebel. God did not design the old self to go to Church, attend self-help groups, memorize Scripture, or be a part of a cell group for transformation. These things in themselves are good, but it will not alter or transform the old self. Derek Prince says somewhere within his teaching, The Old Self and New Self mp3, that religion is like a refrigerator, it can temporarily hide corruption, but it cannot ultimately change it. Somewhere in his teaching he says, and I paraphrase, religion is like a piece of fruit, it looks good, ripe, and appetizing. Yet, if left in the refrigerator, it will ultimately rot. Why? The process of corruption is already at work within the fruit. We can incarcerate or slowdown that process of corruption by refrigeration. But because of corruption, that piece of fruit that started to grow on that vine or tree was birthed to die if not eaten. Quite a few Christian lives remind me of this process. They go to Church and yet do not taking advantage of crucifying the old self. The Church can incarcerate religion, or conceal it, but it in the end cannot change it. Self-realization, the law, and religion cannot change the old self.

"So every good tree bears good fruit, but the bad tree bears bad fruit. A good tree cannot produce bad fruit, nor can a bad tree produce good fruit. Every tree that does not bear good fruit is cut

down and thrown into the fire. So then, you will know them by their fruits." Matthew 7:17-20 NASB

Jesus is using a tree as an example of the two selves, the fallen part of man and the future regeneration or the born again man. Paul has labelled them as the old self and the new self. The old self cannot produce good fruit, and so in turn, the new self cannot produce bad fruit. The old self or that tree must be cut down. What was Jesus referring to? In New Testament language, He was referring to crucifixion. The old self must be done away with. There is no remedy for the old self outside of crucifixion. The good news of the gospel tells us that execution has already taken place in Christ. This is what theology calls positional Christianity. As I opened this chapter, this is the key to understanding the gospel message. The key is positional versus conditional Christianity. My condition in this present evil age, the old self, must be taken off, put to death. My new self which is created in Christ Jesus, must be put on, or I must now live according to the leadings and promoting's of the Holy Spirit, and in so doing not fulfilling the desires of the flesh. Let's look at how The Living Bible describes these two selves in Romans 7:21-25:

"It seems to be a fact of life that when I want to do what is right, I inevitably do what is wrong. I love to do God's will so far as my new nature is concerned; but there is something else deep within me, in my lower nature, that is at war with my mind and wins the fight and makes me a slave to the sin that is still within me. In my mind I want to be God's willing servant, but instead I find myself still enslaved to sin."

So you see how it is: my new life tells me to do right, but the old nature that is still inside me loves to sin. Oh, what a terrible predicament I'm in! Who will free me from my slavery to this deadly lower nature? Thank God! It has been done by Jesus Christ our Lord. He has set me free.

Paul is an Apostle, he is born again, infilled with the Holy Spirit, a worker of miracles, healings, and deliverances. Most scholars agree that Romans was written around A.D. 56. Paul was believed to have been put to death about eight years later. My point is that Paul had not attained perfection and is writing about what must take place inside the believer. He is writing about the key or secret to the success of the believer.

Let us examine this text and insert ourselves within. When we want to do right or have a will to do good, do we find another law at work or do we inevitably do wrong? An honest answer is yes! Paul says that when we are doing God's will and loving it, causing delight within, it comes from the inward man or the new nature. The Apostle says he recognizes another spiritual law within his members, something else deep within him, this lower nature. Paul finds these two natures are at war within the mind, bringing him into captivity to the law of sin which he finds in the lower nature, the old self. The old self wins the fight and Paul becomes a slave to sin which is still within the lower nature or old self.

Throughout Paul's journey as a Christian, he speaks here about the power of the believer through the secret of the two natures. Paul says, in my mind I want to be God's willing servant, but instead I find myself still enslaved to sin. So you see how it is: my new life tells me to do right, but the old nature that is still inside me loves to sin. He needs to be delivered from the old self and says, who will free me from my slavery to this deadly lower nature? Thank God! It has been done by Jesus Christ our Lord. He has set me free. Paul's amazing answer is that it was done in Christ Jesus positionally. We have the victory in Christ and the power through the Holy Spirit to crucify the old self. Notice how the New King James closes chapter 7, "So then, with the mind I myself serve the law of God, but with the flesh the law of sin." Romans 8 shows us how the new self is supposed to thrive. Let us look at Romans 6:6-8 on how Jesus has set us free.

"We know that our old sinful selves were crucified with Christ so that sin might lose its power in our lives. We are no longer slaves to sin. For when we died with Christ we were set free from the power of sin. And since we died with Christ, we know we will also live with him."

I have found that most Christians don't know the truth about the old self and the new self. First, Paul reveals positional Christianity by stating that those who are born again were crucified with Christ. This is also called substitutional Christianity. Simply put, Jesus died in my place, so I'm to believe and no longer live for myself. When Paul states that the body of sin, the old self, might be done away with, that is conditional. Might is a word that expresses possibility! It means there is a sanctification process that must be invoked. Paul says that as we go through sanctification, sin loses its power. Positionally, we have the new self, which is free from sin's power and not enslaved to sin. Verse 7 states that he who has died—died to what?—the old self. We believe that we shall (present/future) live with Him. So, the only way of escape from the slavery of sin is to crucify the old lower nature called the old man. Because of Jesus, we don't have to be enslaved by the lower nature. I will not argue concerning the two selves, only the Holy Spirit can give insight and revelation on the subject of these two natures. Our old self is the criminal.

In closing this chapter, God's solution for the old man is execution so that the power of sin will no longer bring the believer into captivity but into freedom through the born again new man that the Holy Spirit regenerated by way of Jesus' crucifixion, burial, and resurrection.

Recapping, the old self is the product of deception, that is, of Satan's lie. That which denies the truth of God's Word. Deception then gave birth to lust, perverted damaging desires. When one yields to lust, it produces sin, and sin, when it takes its course, produces death. This is the scriptural degenerative process of the old man. The old man has two distinctive characteristics: first, it is corrupt (spiritually, morally, and physically); and secondly, it is a rebel.

2 - The New Man
A creative act of God

In our last chapter, I dealt on the origin and nature of the old self. We concluded that the old self is the product of deception, that is, of Satan's lie; that which denies the truth of God's Word. Deception then gave birth to lust, perverted damaging desires. When one yields to lust, it produces sin, and sin, when it takes its course, produces death. This is the scriptural degenerative process of the old man. The old man has two distinctive characteristics: first, it is corrupt (spiritually, morally, and physically), and secondly, it is a rebel. So, the old self responds to deception, the product of a lie. Deception is the action, through a lie, that deceives or causes us to believe a lie. Deception produces evil lusts that causes sin which leads to death eventually. Let us look at our scripture from Ephesians:

"that you put off, concerning your former conduct, the old man which grows corrupt according to the deceitful lusts, and be renewed in the spirit of your mind, and that you put on the new man which was created according to God, in true righteousness and holiness." Ephesians 4:22-24 NKJV

In this chapter, I am going to explain the nature and origin of the new man. Again from our scripture, we can plainly see our old self and our new self. This is something that cannot be argued or theologically explained away. This is sound Bible doctrine or as the definition states, a set of beliefs held to and taught by Scripture. Those that deny the lower nature inside have fallen into deception.

We see from our scripture four main aspects of the new man. First, it is produced from a creative act of God, the born again creation. This is something humanity cannot do on its own. Jesus in John 3 says, Spirit (Holy Spirit) gives birth to spirit (human spirit). Any act of man cannot produce the creative regeneration of the human spirit. Religion fails, as does good works or legalism, the new man is a creative act of God. This creative act of God proceeds out of the truth, only out of the truth of God's Word. This process is the exact opposite of how death came through the lie. From our scripture, we see there is a nature produced in the new man, this nature is righteousness and holiness. Paul says, this new man is in the likeness of God. The new man is according to the purpose of God. God's purpose or His reason for which He created the new man is about His likeness. It was God's determination to bring about His creation for which the new man exists, His original purpose for creating mankind.

The new man is the idea, the thought, and suggestion of the original purpose for man. Man was to reflect God's likeness and man was to be God's expression. Jesus being the last Adam, the end of something, has set forth God's likeness in Himself. Jesus is God's expression of God's glory and nature. Jesus, the incarnation, expressed the very thought and feelings of God in words and deeds. It is in Jesus that the new self is restoring the likeness of God throughout the earth.

"Do not lie to one another, for you have stripped off the old (unregenerate) self with its evil practices, and have clothed yourselves with the new [spiritual self], which is [ever in the process

of being] renewed and remolded into [fuller and more perfect knowledge upon] knowledge after the image (the likeness) of Him Who created it." Colossians 3:9-10 AMP

Paul says that lying is the root manifestation or the expression of the old self. All lies have their origin in Satan and, thus, he is a liar by nature. Paul goes on to say, put on the new self who is being renewed to a true and perfect knowledge according to the image or likeness of God who is the creator of the new self.

Colossians states, the new self is being remolded or progressively renewed. When we look back at Ephesians 4, Paul is emphasizing the act of creation, but in Colossians, Paul stresses the process of being renewed. We can conclude from both Ephesians and Colossians the special importance Paul is wanting his readers to focus in on. Not only the creation of the new man, but the process of sanctification of the new man. If we lose focus of these two points Paul is emphasizing, then we can be led astray, and be in doctrinal error.

Sanctifications first meaning is that of being set apart to God. This happens when we become born again, God's creative act of regenerating the human spirit of those who accept Christ as Lord and Savior. Sanctification also implies a course of life that befits one's salvation, and this is the process: the process is of the separation of evil things by the believer. Paul is stating, this is the will of God. Just as the truth of God's Word gave birth, so it is the gospel that calls, and the believer who must learn as it teaches. It is the Apostles directive for the new man to first come back into the true knowledge of God and secondly, Paul uses the image of his creator, the new man reflecting God's likeness. So the new man is being progressively renewed, and secondly, fulfilling the two end purposes of God—the true knowledge of God and the restoration of God's image or likeness through holiness.

The New Man Manufactured

What does the Bible say about how the new man is produced? Ephesians 4:24 says, he is created by a birth. Created is the operative word. In the gospel of John, in chapter 3, verses 3-8, Jesus speaks of being born again. Theology uses the word regeneration. Regeneration is a secret act of God in which He imparts new spiritual life to us. John 1:13 incorporate the statement "born of God." In the work of regeneration, we play no active role, it is totally a work of God. John 1:13 specifically says that those who are children of God are born of God. Ezekiel 36:26-27 references the old man and new man:

I will give you a new heart and put a new spirit in you; I will remove from you your heart of stone and give you a heart of flesh. And I will put my Spirit in you and move you to follow my decrees and be careful to keep my laws. Ezekiel 36:26-27 NIV

God's sovereign work in regeneration is what He promises through the prophetic word of Ezekiel that, in the future, He would give new spiritual life to those who accept Christ's work of atonement. It is God working as the third person of the trinity, the Holy Spirit, to produce regeneration. Like 1 Peter 1:23,

"For you have been born again, not of perishable seed, but of imperishable, through the living and enduring word of God." From Ezekiel, it was the prophetic word, and from Peter, it is the written word, yet both have their source in God. When God speaks, the exact relationship in time between regeneration and the proclamation of the gospel is difficult to define, but God is effectively calling man to salvation through His Word. Let me say it this way, when God speaks, He is effectively calling or summoning to Himself a people that receive a new spiritual life through regeneration.

The New Testament is very clear on the spiritual position of the old man and new man. The old man is dead, and produces works of death. But the new man is spiritually alive, is living for God, and produces works of righteousness and holiness. As we receive God's Word by faith and obey it, God's Spirit brings forth within us the very nature of God. As Derek Prince would say somewhere in his teachings, divine, incorruptible, and eternal.

We are talking about how the new man is produced or manufactured. I use the word manufactured because it gives the idea of something that is progressively built. There is a beginning, and it starts with being born again. This new creation, is also built. It is designed and through a process of construction, it is made to be a reflection or an image of God, in truth, righteousness, and holiness.

The new self is incorruptible, it is the very nature of God coming out of the Word of God. That seed of the preached

Word of God, or the Living Word of God [Jesus] received and believed brings forth the nature and the person of God, Jesus.

I have been crucified with Christ; it is no longer I who live, but Christ lives in me; and the life which I now live in the flesh I live by faith in the Son of God, who loved me and gave Himself for me. Galatians 2:20 NKJV

We can now see the two selves so clearly. Paul says God's program for the old self is crucifixion in Christ, but also an ongoing crucifixion, that is, the life Paul lives in the flesh. To live by faith, Paul says, is to put the Word of God to work and let it build within us the new man, that is, form the image of God within. We go nowhere until the old self is executed. Our old self was crucified on the cross with Christ and Paul says it is now Christ who is living in him, not living for the old self. This is called positional and conditional Christianity. Positionally, my old self was crucified in Christ on the cross, but conditionally, my old man is going through a death process. The key to the New Testament is to understand that positionally I live in Christ and have the power to say no to sin through God's grace. As long as we live in this evil age, the sin nature or the old man will always be a reminder of how evil sin really is. It is God's design in this age that man has a connection with sin, so that we can truly see how harmful sin is. Each believer must understand the correct New Testament teaching on justification, sanctification, and glorification.

How To Develop The New Man

Paul says in Ephesians 4:23, there is something we must do. He says that we must be renewed in the spirit of our mind. In order to put off the old self, there must be a total change in the mind, in the way we think. What Paul is proclaiming is becoming a different person entirely, to be transformed on the inside into the likeness of Jesus. The old self is a child of the devil; it was produced out of deceit. Deceit or deception activates lusts, and when we act on lusts, these harmful desires, it brings forth death. The new man has the ability in Christ Jesus to alter the agreements the old self has made with evil. The new self has been born of God, he is a child of God, and through the transformed mind, he moves from darkness to light. Paul explains these two selves so powerfully in Romans, chapters 6-8. In the new spiritual birth, sin's power over us was broken. Spiritually we became part of Christ Jesus through His death and resurrection. Through Jesus' death, the sinful nature was broken, but not done away with. We could say, it was mortally wounded, powerless, if you will, to the new man. We have become a part of Christ—we positionally died with Him, and now we positionally share His new life through our born again spirit. Positionally, our old evil desires through the old self have been nailed to the cross in Christ, judged, crushed, and fatally wounded. This happened so that our sin loving old self is no longer under sin's control. We who are spiritual know that sin is a person, and that person and his kingdom have been sinning from the beginning. The new man no longer needs to be a slave to sin.

For when we are controlled by the new nature, the new man, we have become deaden to sin's power and control. We have become freed from all its passions that lure or lust, and this is what it means to be free from sin's power over us. Paul reveals, since our old self died with Christ positionally, we know that our new self will share in His life. We see sanctification here. This is what Paul is saying about the renewing of the mind. The renewed mind understands that death no longer has power through the old self, because the new self begins to live a life of unbroken fellowship with God.

The transformation of the mind starts when we look upon our old sinful nature and its passions and desires as dead, no longer pulling on us. We could say, we are now unresponsive to sin. The new self is alive to God, alert and responsive to the Holy Spirit, through our new life in Christ Jesus. The mind of the new self will not allow sin to control the body any longer. It will not give in to sinful desires, and refuses the old self to become instruments or tools of wickedness, thereby glorifying sin's power. The new self is given over completely to God. The mind of the new self says, every part of creation, spirit, soul, and body, is obedient to the Spirit of God as instruments of righteousness or to be used for God's purpose.

The new creation [new self] says, I will never be enslaved again by sin through the old self. It says that sin will not be my master because I am no longer tied to laws that bring death, where sin was empowered. The mind of the new self says, I am free through Christ, empowered over the old self and sin, and completely under the control of the Holy Spirit, experiencing

God's favor and mercy. This is why the believer can no longer willfully sin. Choosing to willfully sin surrenders to the old self which is empowered by sin and makes us surrender to that person, sin, as master. God's grace shown in the new created man will not keep on sinning. The transformed mind of the new created self says, if I can't say no to that person of sin, I will be delivered through Christ. Deliverance is the only option. The new self understands the laws of God, and realizes I can give in to the old self and death or I can choose obedience and be acquitted.

As one who has done thousands of exorcisms, if we chose to obey sin, we obey a spiritual person of evil. The Bible says, to the one to whom we offer ourselves, he will take you and become your master. This means we allow through the old self to be enslaved to that evil spirit being.

Through God's creation of the new self, we now obey with our hearts the gospel to which God has committed us. As the new self begins to reign, conditionally, we are being set free from our old self, no longer under his mastery and his power of sin. But through the new self, we have a new master, Christ Jesus, and we reign and rule through righteousness and holiness. Paul is writing this way, using illustrations of slaves and masters, because it is easy to picture and so understand. In Christ, we are to be slaves to all that is right and holy, exhibiting and reflecting God's image and likeness.

The mind of the new self, desires exposure or to be exposed to contact with the Holy Spirit. I chose the word exposure because it means experiencing a condition, identity, or fact. In Romans 12:2, Paul says the new man will learn from exposure how God's ways really are, and through them we will be satisfied. The mind of the new self says look, the behavior and customs of this world or evil age is not to be obeyed. It is the Holy Spirit working through the new self that brings to us the truth. He teaches us how to overcome the old self, and in so doing, defeat the powers of sin, and the evil spirit beings that rule this evil age. To be conformed to this world is to let the old self have his way in our lives. To be transformed, is to yield to the new self who is empowered by the Holy Spirit. The new self is seeking the will of God, which is the development and maturing of the new self. To develop means to go through a process of growth and advancement, being refined into the likeness and image of Christ Jesus. To mature is to grow up in our salvation: going through stages of thought, reaching for the most advanced stages of the new self, as our mind is renewed to God's will. We can understand this or take it one step further in Ephesians 1:18.

I pray that the eyes of your heart may be enlightened, so that you will know what is the hope of His calling, what are the riches of the glory of His inheritance in the saints. Ephesians 1:18 NASB

We see Paul tell the believer what further needs to happen in this transformation of the mind and the new self. Notice, it is the Holy Spirit who is to flood our hearts with light or truth, so that we can see the hope of our calling, the full development of the new self and its destiny. Through our development, as we advance in our calling or the maturing of the new self, we participate in the future or the power of the age to come, in which we were called to share. There is a day coming when the new self will be fully manifested, that day will come at the resurrection. Paul says, flesh and blood or the old self cannot enter the Kingdom of God (1 Corinthians 15:50). Our bodies must undergo a transformation so that they are no longer made up of flesh and blood, but a spiritual body. The old self who has the nature of Satan, which is also made up of flesh and blood and is corrupted by sin will die, this is part of the curse. It is also a witness for the believer today, to no longer allow the old self to reign in our mortal bodies.

We know that judgment will terminate this evil age and bring the sons of the Kingdom into their full inheritance of the Kingdom, that is, the completion of the new self. What will happen at the end of this sinful age, Jesus says the angels will come and separate the evil from the righteous. Those who have chosen to live from the new self will be glorified and shine like the sun in the Kingdom of God. Those who have lived by the old self, have never really known God, they will be thrown into the fiery furnace where there will be weeping and gnashing of teeth. It is from the new self that we come to know God. Paul says our hearts have been in darkness and it is the Holy Spirit who brings to our hearts the light of truth.

When Jesus returns at the end of this evil age (Revelations 19:11-16) and before the age to come (Revelations 21:1) there is an interval when the saints are raised to reign with Christ for a thousand years. This is when the new self will be fully manifested, at the Millennium. The Church age is the period of

Christ's invisible glory, so the new self is concealed. Paul says in Philippians 3 that he had given up everything, dying to the old self, so that he could come to really know Christ and to experience the mighty power through the new self or, as the Living Bible states, brought him back to life again. Paul said he had not been made perfect or the new creation perfected, but he would keep working toward that day when he would finally be all that Christ recreated him to be.

The Millennium will be the period of the manifested glory of Christ and all those who have believed in Him. The glorification of the new self will be a witness of the triumphant Kingdom of God within history, the Millennium. The Millennium is the reign of the visible Christ, so the age to come [eternity] is the reign of the Father. It is scripturally called the age to come. At that time, the age to come, there will be the resurrection of the dead, those who lived governed by the old self, and the destruction of the gods of the evil age. Revelations 20 speaks of two resurrections, one at the beginning of the Millennium and a second resurrection at the end of the Millennium. We also find stages in the conquest over Satan and the fallen angels. When Jesus returns at the end of this evil age and the Millennium starts, Satan and his angels are thrown into the abyss and chained for a thousand years. You need to follow me very closely here. Jesus' return is the glorification of the new self for those that have believed while this evil age lasted. At the end of the Millennium, Satan and his fallen angels are released to engage in their wicked, sinful activities again. Some of mankind will survive the tribulation and enter the Millennium, and even though Christ is ruling, the old self within them will be responsive to evil and the attractions of evil through the old self, and rebel against Christ. How does that happen? The old self responds to its father's will. We ask, how powerful is the old man? When the glorified Christ is reigning in glory and power during the Millennium, Satan and the fallen angels will still find hearts of men who have refused salvation and are still responsive to sin through the old self.

This is why the Holy Spirit has to bring to us the light of truth. It is only through the truth that we can see what God has for us in the new self. What we can't forget and that is vital to the growth of the new self is the Holy Spirit working through the mirror of the Word of God. As our minds are renewed, the new self, the new creation operates from the age to come. Today, we have the choice to obey the message of God's Word, not just listen to it. Don't fall prey to the old self, for if we just listen and not obey, we are looking into a mirror which reflects the new man, but if we walk away, and forget, we can't see the new man anymore. This is what James is referring to. But, if we steadily look into God's Word, we will remember and do what it says and be transformed into Christ's likeness. We are blessed by God as the new man is developed. James says, the Word of God is a mirror that is held up before us. The new self is reflected in that mirror, but some will walk away and disregard that likeness, follow after the old man, and perish. This is the lukewarm believer! Destined for destruction! Some on the other hand will look into the law of liberty, freedom from the old self, looking intently, and abide by it, this is the believer who lives in this evil age blessed. So the mirror is revealing what God's grace desires for the new self, freedom!

Now the Lord is the Spirit; and where the Spirit of the Lord is, there is liberty. but we all, with unveiled face, beholding as in a mirror the glory of the Lord, are being transformed into the same image from glory to glory, just as by the Spirit of the Lord. 2 Corinthians 3:17-18 NKJV

Paul says, the Lord is the Spirit, and where God's Spirit is, the new man is, and there is freedom. Through the new creation, the veil has been removed and we can see through the new self and, in so doing, reflect the glory of the Lord. The reflection of God is through the development of the new self as he is transformed. Notice the transformation of the new self into the same image as the Lord, going from glory to glory, just as the Holy Spirit makes us more and more like Jesus. The image of God is restored through the new self, and it is a process of ongoing victory. Notice, the one who is working this process is the Holy Spirit. Yet He only works as we are looking into the mirror of God's Word, desiring obedience.

There is one more important principle we cannot leave out in connection, and it is this, the new man grows at the cost of the old man. The new self tastes and sees that this new life is what is fulfilling, and says, Jesus must increase and I must decrease. Let us say it this way, the new man in Christ must increase and the old man created in the likeness of Satan must decrease. What I am implying is, only in proportion to the willingness of the death of my old self will my new self grow! There has to be a death, if there is going to be a new life. A couple of key points here, we must accept what God says about the old man, and it must be crucified. Positionally, the old man was crucified with

Christ, Romans 6:6, and conditionally, we must consider ourselves dead to the power of sin, Romans 6:11. These are two facts that must be received by faith since it is the Word of God. Many writers and theologians can't accept these two scriptural facts! Again, the first fact is, positionally, the old sinful selves were crucified and second, conditionally, we are not to let sin control the way we live by giving in to sin's desires. We are not to let any part of our body become an instrument of evil to serve sin (Romans 6:12-13). Paul says the old self will want to go on acting as if he has rights. We are not to give in, but to live from the new self which is alive in Christ Jesus. The new self presents himself to the Holy Spirit by yielding its members. What gives the Holy Spirit access? Obedience. These are the facts, and this is correct theology. So, we must examine the truth of God's Word and let it reveal the two natures—what we were by nature, the old self, and what we can become by grace, the new self. We must systematically deny the desires of the old self and yield to the influence of the Holy Spirit. The result can be expressed in one word of our conduct—obedience.

God's Agenda for the New Self

To understand God's purpose for the new man, we must realize that when God arranged a purpose for man, He never gives up on it. So we must start at the beginning. From Scripture, we learn that sin and Satan may delay God's reason for which man was created, but both can never ultimately thwart it. The new man was created in righteousness, holiness, and truth. The new man's home is the age to come. The new man doesn't belong to this evil age, it doesn't like sin, sickness, and suffering. At the coming of Christ, when the righteous are raised, the new man will experience the fullness of the Kingdom of God. The new self has the ability to receive the blessings of the future age in the present. Christ gave Himself for our sins to deliver us from the present evil age. How can mankind who lives in this present evil age be delivered from its power? The deliverance comes through the power of the age to come and living through the new man.

For it is impossible [to restore and bring again to repentance] those who have been once for all enlightened, who have consciously tasted the heavenly gift and have become sharers of the Holy Spirit, and have felt how good the Word of God is and the mighty powers of the age and world to come, if they then deviate from the faith and turn away from their allegiance—[it is impossible] to bring them back to repentance, for (because, while, as long as) they nail upon the cross the Son of God afresh [as far as they are concerned] and are holding [Him] up to contempt and shame and public disgrace. Hebrews 6:4-6 AMP

Because of the power of the two natures, those inward characteristics that are graphed in the chemical make up of the person, the inherited qualities, if at one time a person becomes born again, regenerated, but returns to the world, it is of no use trying to bring them back to the Lord again. The key phrase of the writer to the Hebrews and the great divide in the body of Christ's theology, if the person has understood repentance, the power within the new man over sin, experienced the ongoing process of the transformation of the new man, the presence and power of Christ Jesus in them through the Holy Spirit, if they turn back to that indwell lower natures, the old man, to bring them back to repentance. I've seen very true conversions, touches of the Holy Spirit, but thousands have not understood, and turned back because the old man loves the world.

Some schools of thought would like to say, the person who walks away from the Lord was never really saved. These schools of thought will say, once saved, always saved. They quote 1 John 2:19:

They went out from us [seeming at first to be Christians], but they were not really of us [because they were not truly born again and spiritually transformed]; for if they had been of us, they would have remained with us; but they went out [teaching false doctrine], so that it would be clearly shown that none of them are of us. 1 John 2:19 AMP

In balancing these scriptures of Hebrews and John properly, the secret is found in the old man and new man. Hebrew 6 says that they once understood the gospel. This comes in line with 1 John 2 where he says "seeming to be Christians". They tasted of the good things of heaven and the Holy Spirit, even knowing the Word of God. We must stop right here, if someone belongs to the world, they can never taste of the powers of heaven, because they are not born again and belong to the devil. The Bible clearly teaches that a man must be born again to enter or taste of the Kingdom of God, the power of the age to come. And to enter the Kingdom of God, one must be regenerated. What is John really saying in balance with Jesus and Hebrews? He is saying that such a person never allowed the born again experience to impact their life or to take root and grow, much like Matthew 13. 1 John 2:19, looking at this scripture on the surface and if it stood alone, we would have to conclude that the person never really got saved. This is in direct contradiction with Jesus' teaching in John 3 about entering the Kingdom through the born again experience. Hebrews even says they have turned against God. You can't turn against God unless you have turned to God.

As we turn back to God's agenda, in Ephesians 1:11, Paul says, because of what Christ has done, we have a destiny, claimed by God as His own, for an inheritance, having been predestined or chosen beforehand according to God's purpose in Christ who works everything according to His counsel and the design of His will. Everything is coming in line with God's purpose and will. This is in accordance to God's original purpose in creating man. Sin, sickness, even Satan, may have delayed God's plan for man, but cannot ultimately stop it. God will ultimately work out His purpose and His plan. This plan is so clearly portrayed in what the New Testament says about the old self and the new self. In Genesis 1:26-28, the Bible reveals what God did in Christ and so elegantly brought forward in the New Testament. Genesis is talking about mankind, not just one individual man. Let us look at the two main purposes of God in the creation of humanity. Man is to reflect God's likeness, because he is made in God's image and likeness. God did not rest until He brought forth His likeness in the creation. The second purpose in creating man is to exercise God's authority. If man was created in an image, then within that image is authority. Man was to rule over all the earth on God's behalf. Psalm 115:16 confirms man's rule in the interests of God.

Man's authority is found as he rules as God would rule, exercising God's authority over all the earth.

When man sinned, it frustrated both of God's purposes for man. We see that God's image and likeness was spoiled, and man became a slave. Jesus came and restored God's image and likeness by stating in John 14:9, "if you have seen Me, then you have seen the Father." This is the revelation of the new man's likeness and authority. In John 14:10, Jesus says that it is the Father who abided in Him that does the work. Jesus is saying that the words and works are from the Father's authority.

In John 20:21, so Jesus said to them again, "Peace to you! As the Father has sent Me, I also send you." In the same way the Father sent Jesus and in the victories Jesus attained, so are we to go through the new creation. Jesus came in the authority of the Father, now we through the new man go in that same authority through Christ Jesus. This is so important to understand. Our authority as a believer is in understanding how the Kingdom of God operates, this only comes through the new self.

Jesus came to fulfill the purposes of the Father which Adam through his fall was unable to do. Sin brought about the old self which was and is unable to follow or be successful in fulfilling God's plan for mankind. The new man now can reveal God's likeness again and can exercise God's authority. Jesus has paved the way for all to go and do as He did.

For those whom He foreknew, He also predestined to become conformed to the image of His Son, so that He would be the firstborn among many brethren; Romans 8:29 NASB

This is a perfect scripture for God's destiny of the new self. Paul is describing God's purpose for the new man and uses the word conformed. It means to make of like-form or "to bring to the same form with" some other person or thing, "to render like." The noun morphē refers to the outward expression of an inward essence or nature. Thus, in the process of sanctification, the saint is transformed in his inner heart life to resemble the Lord Jesus. The new self being transformed into the image, likeness, with authority, as he grows in nature of Christ Jesus. Notice it was God's purpose to bring forth many children of Jesus' likeness.

In closing this chapter, we are to exercise Christ's authority on His behalf.

And Jesus came up and spoke to them, saying, "All authority has been given to Me in heaven and on earth. Go therefore and make disciples of all the nations, baptizing them in the name of the Father and the Son and the Holy Spirit, teaching them to observe all that I commanded you; and lo, I am with you always, even to the end of the age." Matthew 28:18-20 NASB

After Jesus' resurrection, He says, all authority belongs to Him, and He now sends us in the power of the transformed new self. We go on Jesus' behalf to exercise authority with demonstrations of power as His representatives. Making disciples is expressed as believers teaching and modeling how to execute the old self, and release the new self in the power of Christ Jesus. What we teach is the delegated authority of the Lord Jesus Christ.

And one more last point that is of great importance! The purpose of God in bringing forth many children is to bring a collective body of believers as one new man as stated in Ephesians 2:14-15.

For He Himself is our peace, who made both groups into one and broke down the barrier of the dividing wall, by abolishing in His flesh the enmity, which is the Law of commandments contained in ordinances, so that in Himself He might make the two into one new man, thus establishing peace, Ephesians 2:14-15 NASB

God's overall purpose for the new man is a body of believers operating as one new man. This cannot happen unless the Church turns back to the Holy Spirit. God's design is for the new man to operate through a corporative body, the Church, to bring forth His likeness and authority. Notice Ephesians 4:16, from whom the whole body, being fitted and held together by what every joint supplies, according to the proper working of each individual part, causes the growth of the body for the building up of itself in love. We are to be one complete corporate body, expressing one new corporate man. This new man is to reenact Christ's earthly ministry and in so doing fulfills God's two purposes, revealing God to the world and exercises God's authority in Christ Jesus.

3 - The War of Natures
Romans 5:12-8:39

What most people don't see in theological passages in the Bible, such as we are looking at, is the supernatural behind the theology. As we examine the death in the old man through Adam and life in the new man through Christ Jesus; dead to sin and alive in Christ; the old man a slave, the new man free through righteousness; the war inside between the old and new man and our life, power, and glorification through the Holy Spirit, I will attempt to bring out the supernatural as we progress through the salvation to freedom texts. We will see how the power of God has and is dealing with our position in Christ and our condition in Adam.

Paul starts out by saying that when Adam sinned, he engaged in wrongdoing by willfully and morally transgressing God's law. He was acting contrary to God's will by choosing to go in an opposite direction to the way and course God had chosen for him. By choosing to obey Satan, Adam gave himself and humanity over to a governing principle where fundamentally we would live from a system of beliefs and behavior that would start chains of reason that is rooted and established in lies. Adam would find another nature working within his body that had power over him, and it brought forth sin. Sin would now have a seat, a permanent residence, in the will of man. Man would recognize sins seat because it would manifest itself in the conscience of humanity. Sin's power would be seen through human choices as he allowed his body to become an instrument for evil. Adam would now determine what he considered lawful or not. Adam would no longer by nature have the ability to fulfill God's law. As long as we, the new creation, are trapped in our human body, the flesh, sins indwelling presence, will continually produce lawlessness. Sin's nature comes from Satan and the fallen angels. If Satan, a metaphor for the fallen, have been sinning from the beginning, then it would be reasonable to say, the satanic principal indwells the old man, since we also sin. When Satan and the fallen rebelled, they contracted a judgment from God spoken over them throughout the ages upon ages. When Adam sinned, God spoke a curse over him but also said He would redeem mankind through Christ Jesus.

When Adam sinned, sin entered the world or the entire human race and mankind began to sin. His sin spread death throughout all the created universe, so everything began to grow old and die. In Hebrews 1, the writer says God's throne is forever and He rules in righteousness. God created the heavens and the earth, but they will come to an end, they will all wear out like a garment, You (God) will roll them up like a robe and they will be changed like clothes. The creation waits in eager expectation when God does away with sin and the sons of God are fully revealed. When Paul says that death came from sin, he is talking about a process of dying. Sin brought immediate spiritual death, but physical death would be a process. Let me just add here, the laws of God we break through the sinful nature bring spiritual consequences just as it did with Adam and Eve. These consequences could result in demonization, curses, sicknesses.

Paul reminds us that people sinned even before the law was

given. People who lived between the time of Adam to Moses did not have any specific laws to break. Sin is first a person, then it is a power, thirdly, it is an act. Sin was in the world from the beginning, but it came into sharp focus when the law was given. Mankind began to perceive or become aware within the conscious and through his sense see a power that took advantage through the old man. It's desires to do evil wanted to grow and become further independent of God. Let me give us a realization that any student of the Bible faces in this book, the awareness that evil indwells the old man as visualized through physical death. The law of Moses still today, as it did in the Old Testament, help people see their sinfulness. The law shows us the seriousness of our offenses, and to drive us to Christ for salvation and the forgiveness of sins. For Paul to write about this means that in his day it was still true. So the law points out our sin and places the responsibility for it on us. The law has no remedy; it just identifies the problem.

The contrast between Adam and Christ is the manifestation of the two selves, the old and new man. Adam's transgression determined his nature and character for a time; Christ's one act of righteousness determined a nature and character for eternity. When Paul mentions the gift, he is talking about justification through salvation in Christ Jesus. The opposite is found in the Adamic nature—condemnation. Death is the revelator of God's judgment on the sinful nature of man. Eternal life belongs to the new creation, the spirit and the soul. As we pursue righteousness, the new man, God's design for humanity, starts to produce good works that God has designed from the beginning. Remember what Paul is describing concerning the old man. The old self is the product of deception, that is, of Satan's lie. That which denies the truth of God's Word. Deception then gave birth to lust, perverted damaging desires. When one yields to lust it produces sin, and sin, when it takes its course, produces death. This is the scriptural degenerative process of the old man. The old man has two distinctive characteristics: first, it is corrupt (spiritually, morally, and physically), and secondly, it is a rebel. This happened when God passed judgment on Adam's one sin of disobedience. This degenerative process has affected the entire human race and brought condemnation. Paul takes this process one step further in Romans 5:17 stating that Adam caused death to rule over the whole human race. What the underlying point here is, death will rule over this evil age. But God's gift of righteousness through salvation in Christ Jesus takes us spiritually out of the realms of darkness and the control of the fallen angels and sets us free spiritually. We see the power of the new man in Christ as our minds are freed from the fallen angels through not being conformed to the pattern of this evil age or world. Conformed here means to be or become behaviorally or socially similar to the characteristics of the world. As our mind becomes set free from the fallen angels, the Holy Spirit begins to reestablish a mind responsive to Christ. The Holy Spirit desires to bring the mind of the one born again into glorification. To lift the mind into higher spheres, to enlarge the borders of meaning and truth. The renewed mind by the Holy Spirit starts to experience far deeper thought, mightier truths, and to express spiritual power.

When Adam sinned, mankind came under its power. The fallen angels having control within the old man's nature brought forth disobedience and condemnation. Sin has always brought forth heartache and punishment. Yet Christ's one act of righteousness, dying on the cross for the sins of the world, opened the way for all people to be made right in God's sight and to undergo sanctification. Sanctification is where the old nature lives no more and the believer starts to live by the new creation, the new man. So the law was given to the Jews and for the whole human race, so that all people could see how sinful they are. Paul's argument in the first five chapters of Romans is that the law has made mankind aware of their need for salvation and to be delivered from the power of sin. We all know that this age is characterized by sin and a kingdom of evil who's power over the human race is sin; this inevitably brings death, but death can also be manifested in areas of human life. Christ's bodily death and resurrection has positioned the believer to reign over sin and the evil powers of sin, bringing the believer into victory and eternal life. I have chosen these biblical chapters so that the believer can see positional and conditional Christianity.

Romans 6

In reading Romans, chapters 1-5, Paul has shown people's need for salvation, the sin nature of humanity, sin, and its power reigning over humanity. Paul reveals the need for salvation and the forgiveness of sins. In these next chapters we will see God's program for progressively separating believers from sin and its power and through the new man, making the believer more like Christ. Paul's key point will be that the believer has now another nature working within, the new man. The point will expand to the empowerment of the new man who is found in the Holy Spirit. In chapters 6-7 Paul's focus will be the new nature against the old nature. Paul will show theologically how the kingdom of God through the Holy Spirit works within the believer and also how the kingdom of darkness works at the same time through the satanic principle, sin. Paul reveals that within the born again believer two kingdoms coexist and are at war within, hence, my title of this chapter.

Paul opens chapter six of Romans by saying, we should not take God's wonderful kindness in forgiving sin to keep on willfully sinning. How God shows the believer more and more kindness is His grace through sanctification. Paul's point is, God's grace must not become an excuse to sin and to live immorally. We have died to sin positionally, and Paul says to tap the power of God's grace and be delivered from sin and the old man that sin operates through. Paul leaves open the idea that someone would claim to believe and yet plan on yielding to sin.

What is Paul's theological and spiritual concepts in chapters 6-7? In a legal sense and in a spiritual sense, the believer has died to sin. Through baptism, that is spiritually being buried with Christ. We have died with Christ, and through Christ's resurrection we have been spiritually given a new life. Paul also says that in a moral since, sinful desires will be present, but they have been mortally wounded. The old man is powerless against the work of the Holy Spirit through the new man. Paul is saying the new man has the ability again to reflect the image and likeness of God. This only takes place as the believer learns to live from their position in Christ, disarming the fallen angels, principalities, and powers in the heavenly realm.

Baptism is a metaphor or an analogy of a spiritual truth. We know from scriptural foundations that baptism is an act of a believer who has decided to follow Christ. Paul pictures how Jesus died for sin, we positionally also died to a sinful lifestyle, so that the power of the Holy Spirit can produce in us the new creation and lifestyle. Going under the water is a powerful picture. It is spiritually a picture of Jesus breaking the powers of the fallen angels and demons over the believer's life positionally. This is why many times when a person is baptized by power ministries, deliverance and healings take place. The baptized person comes up out of the water speaking in a heavenly language. So positionally the believer has the power to be free, but conditionally through the flesh, there is a nature and power that must be executed. Theologically, baptism represents the death of the old man and that way of life. It represents being raised in Christ to a new life like His.

Christ's agony of death and His glorious resurrection united us in Him and then coming to the understanding that dying to sin is going to be painful and a lifelong process. Being raised with Christ is more than a theological fact, it is the recreating power of God at work. Authority will always be seen in power. The believer who exercises their position over their condition is the believer who is putting to death the old man, and living in power through the new man.

We do divide the Word of God scripturally as long as it is balanced with power. Jesus' death rendered sin powerless. Power is a person just as sin is a nature. We must never lose spiritual realities as we venture through theological passages in the Bible. Where theology is, so is authority and power. It may not be visible like healing and deliverance, but it is behind the seen upholding theology. For example, when Paul says that through the new man we are no longer slaves to sin, he is speaking positionally. He is saying, we are to exercise our transformed mind over sin or we are to be delivered from persons of sin, in either case, theology and spiritual ministry are working hand in hand. Remember, we do not war against flesh and blood but against spiritual forces of evil without bodies.

Freedom was rare in biblical times except through death. Death brings about a release that cannot be reversed. Paul's spiritual reality is that as we die to sin and its power (person), we are free to live for Christ. Evil spirit's desire control through sin's power, just as the freedom in Christ wherewith the Holy Spirit desires control to bring about God's image and likeness. Evil thoughts and action reveal who the evil spirit is and what he likes. When Jesus died and defeated the kingdom of darkness, evil spirits through sin were rendered powerless as the believer exercises their new man over the old man in all scriptural processes.

When Paul says we have been identified with Christ, he is referring to who and what someone is. This starts in the mind, where the seat of sin is, where the fallen angels have control. As our minds become renewed in Christ, we recognize and distinguish the difference between the new man and the old man. As we come into association with Christ, our identity changes in thought and action. We start to share the same characteristics as Christ. In our minds we desire the things of God because we are no longer yielding our minds to earthly sinful behavior. Paul asks a major question here, if we are dead to sin, how can sin still control us? Theologically, we have died to sin according to the new man, but according to the old man we are constantly being freed from the desire to sin. Spiritually, we are being delivered by our choices or being exorcised from evil.

Authors owe the body of Christ the whole truth, not just writing from either a theological or spiritual perspective, but both. The truth is, if people have any particular desire and have given in to its lustful desires, then deliverance is the only scriptural method for freedom. If we can say no to sin and it's over, then the power of freewill has repelled evil. Because sin has a power within the believer's soul, we will have the compulsion to sin in the body. I, like Paul, desire to be freed from the sinful nature, yet God has chosen the process of sanctification, so I must too. I do understand that our wrestling match with sin is designed to bring about the power of freewill in the new creation. In God's wisdom, this too is part of our glorification. We must understand that as we live in these mortal bodies, the lower nature, we do have the power to no longer let sin control us. Again, if we cannot say no to sin, then an evil spirit through sin must be exorcised. Paul says, because our mortal decaying bodies are dying, revealing that the old man lives under curses, we should not yield to those sinful desires and temptation coming from demons and fallen angels. Our freedom is found as we give ourselves completely to God and use our whole bodies as tools to do what is right. If we have a choice, then we have been given the power of the new life, and the kingdom of darkness can only do what we permit or obey. Paul says that God's desire in Christ Jesus is that sin will not ever again be our master. Master implies a person, and sin manifests a power. We are not subject to the law or bound as prisoners to the law in the new man. Yet the old man is being freed from the law. The law is revealing sin and evil that operates through sin. True reality, the law produces both the proof and the acute awareness of evil spirits through sin, directing and guiding the individuals into sin's captivity. Paul ends this half of the chapter saying that God's grace, God's forgiveness of sin and His willingness to deliver us from evil will overcome as the believer pursues scriptural procedure.

Freedom To Obey God's Spirit

Paul begins this part of Scripture in almost the same way as the last one. He wants us to have no misunderstanding. In a believer's life there are two masters, sin and the evil spirit behind the sin and the Lord Jesus Christ with the power of the Holy Spirit. The law of God has never been against God's grace, but it came alongside to reveal sin, and the power of the person or evil spirit working behind sin's desires and actions.

Verse one and fifteen seem to almost repeat the question and Paul's response is of the same manner. Paul says, willfully sinning will never bring about God's grace or opportunity to exercise more grace. What willfully sinning does is that it reveals the power of sin in the old man and very likely uncover evil spirit behind that sin. This is seen in verse sixteen of chapter six. As Christians, the righteousness or the sinfulness that we obey shows how much we are surrendered to light, darkness, or a little of both. Paul says we are a slave to whomever or whatever we commit ourselves to obey, in the visible or invisible realms.

When sin becomes someone's master, that individual has no power except to obey what it bids through desire and action. But when we choose to obey God, we become slaves of obedience. There are only two choices, obey God and walk out our salvation or obey the devil and live under his bondage. We all were at one time slaves to sin and the devil, since he has been sinning from the beginning. The old man has the nature and desires of the devil, and through deception and lies, leads us into bondage. The new man was a creative act of God that responds to truth, righteousness, and holiness. Let me say it this way, service to sin and the devil leaves us in captivity and death, service to God and truth, leads us into righteousness and eternal life.

The power of the new man is from the Holy Spirit, but there is also an equal power, the Word of God. Paul says that the Word of God acts like a master keeping us free from sin and the power of the kingdom of darkness. We are no longer living as slaves to sin, but living as slaves to righteousness, experiencing the Kingdom of God. In verse nineteen, the old man is weak, vulnerable to the kingdom of darkness that brings spiritual dishonor and possession. When believers are slaves to impurity and lawlessness, two spiritual categories, they are held in bondage through the old man by spiritual forces of wickedness in the heavenly realms and in the terrestrial realms.

It is God's will through the new man to have benefits of the Kingdom immeasurably. These spiritual blessing comes in two levels. The believer who is born again, filled with the Holy Spirit, and speaking in tongues, and is a student and doer of the Word will experience blessing in accordance to living from the new man and how much the old man is not active. The second level is far more of an outpouring of blessing in extreme measure as the believer does the first step, but adds deliverance from the legal rights and curses accrued in their life and past generations. There is a powerful difference between the two, but as evil spirits lose their right to block blessings, this believer receives showers of blessing.

When Paul mentions the law, he is referring to a system of laws, civil statutes, and priestly ordinances within the Mosaic covenant as a means of God's favor or blessing. Simply put, we do not purposely go out and break the law, for God's Word will stand forever. The believer cannot become righteous through the law, but can willfully or through choice be condemned in the old man through the law. How is that possible? The law itself is not evil, but it does tell us what evil is. There is something else the law will do, it will arouse evil desires. Paul says without the law he would not have known what lust or coveting was. We really must be careful when the law says thou shall not. It is through the old man as I have said before that the kingdom of darkness seeks access for possession. So when the Bible says, thou shall not or do not mark your skin with tattoos, through the old man, evil enters for possession. The body becomes demonized and the soul oppressed. Paul said that no sooner had he become aware of that commandment than it awakens from a sleep, if we will, feelings, emotions, and responses forbidden from within him. Whoever stands on the nonsense opinion that evil spirits attach themselves to believers because a Christian cannot have a demon, that one needs to go back to the Bible and the school of the supernatural and gather correct theology. What Paul is saying so argumentatively is that when the law said thou shall not lust, the law introduced him to some of the darkest emotions and desires. Supernaturally, it introduced him too many realms of evil spirits.

The new man realizes the seriousness of the law and the evil spirits of sin and their power through the old man. In second heaven deliverance, I find this truth holds, and through the old man breaking the laws of God, fallen angels accuse us in the courts of heaven. It is through the old man that they have their rights and curses from the creation. If I live a life of pornography and a life for Christ, the old man is alive and evil spirits have me captive. If through the new man I ask Jesus to deliver me from evil, those spirits are exorcised and that part of the old man dies. The new man thrives at the expense of the old man. Sin finds its power through the commandment, there is nothing wrong with the commandment, but sin lives through the old man. Paul treats the law like a legal binding contract from God. He says the law is holy, righteous or right, and good. Believers must understand Paul and the other Apostles concerning the law, it reflects God's nature, character, and His will. The commandment defines sin and also reveals how evil spirits are defeated. Many times I will take someone who has a lot of sexual immorality in their past and in their generations through curse-breaking according to the law of Moses. One thing I have found in dealing with evil spirits, whether Old or New Testament, "it is written" does them in.

The new man loves the laws of God, not for righteousness, but for power and authority in Christ Jesus. The new man desires to follow God's Word, for in it, the new man sees what God's purpose is for him. That purpose brings within destiny, God's image and likeness to rule again in authority. Satan and sin may have frustrated man, but now the new creation in Christ has destiny and purpose with authority and power. This is why Paul cries out, who will rescue me from this body of sin and death.

Struggle With Sin And Evil

We see from the early Church that they held the law of God in high regard. We as the body of Christ mostly have a different view. We say things like, I'm not under the law, as a way or attitude of disrespect or something as treating the law casually. Paul made an effort to clarify between God's holy law, sin, and the new creation. This view is in the proper perspective or viewpoint. If our outlook is not based on those three points, we can quickly fall into doctrinal or supernatural error. We can quickly think that the cross took care of everything and it doesn't really matter what I do, Jesus will forgive. This statement is a half-truth and a half lie. How can we be free from sin in Christ Jesus and continue to openly sin? In Christ, we are spiritually free from sin, that is our position. In the flesh, sin has an indwelling throne in the seat of the human soul. The believer in Christ spiritually is free from the penalty of sin and judgment. The believer is also free spiritually, free from sin's power of the evil spirits. But while still in the flesh, our sinful nature reveals in the body that we are not free from the temptation of evil spirits and sin. The wake-up call to the believer is that Paul never claimed that being under grace and not under law meant that we somehow were above the law. Hard and cold statement, conditionally we are judged by the law, that is conditionally. Spiritually, we are set free from the law and the power of the transformed mind brings this reality into a fallen and evil age. Let me say it this way, the trouble is not God's law, but me. Paul now reveals his own personal dilemma and invites us to look deeper into our own behavior and understanding of the two selves. Paul shows that while we are in this evil age, the fallen angels have power over that lower nature of sin, just as the Holy Spirit has control and power over the born again human spirit.

Paul gives us three powerful lessons he realized in dealing with the old man. One, scriptural knowledge of the law is not the answer. Two, any type of self-determination or effort to want to do right will not bring lasting change. Three, being a Christian does not conditionally wipe out sin and possession of evil spirits. The baptism of the Holy Spirit is not about speaking in tongues, it's for the empowerment to bring sanctification conditionally or in the flesh. The Holy Spirit is the one who sets us free from sin and evil spirits who enter through sin. Paul gets unbelievably real in Romans 7:16-17. He says it is sin, that is the nature of Satan, inside me that makes me do these evil things the law forbids. Paul says there is a conflict inside him, he wants to do what the law requires, but there is this lower sinful nature that prevents him. He is advocating support for understanding the law and not purposely breaking the law and so many believers do.

We realize that our sinful nature is a part of our being and there is nothing holy, righteous, or good in it. Although we belong to Christ and have died to sin positionally, we still conditionally live in a sinful body and a sinful world. Paul describes the person who tries to do good and has the desire to do good, but can't. Paul says, without the Holy Spirit's aid, there will be no process of death to the old man. Paul says believers love God's law and His ways. They should desire and put into action the things God has for them. But this other law at work within the lower nature keeps the believer from many of the blessings of God.

The believer must know that these two powers within, the Holy Spirit and the satanic principal are not equal, but they are both there. The satanic principle dwelling within the human soul and body, must be executed. If the believer cannot say no to sin, then the believer must come to the truth that, through this satanic principle, evil spirits have accessed their body and are working against the Holy Spirit's sanctification process by way of willfully yielding to sin. As long as we are here on earth, our mortal bodies are bodies of death. The soul of the believer is being renewed or, if need be, being expelled of fallen angels who have access by nature.

The struggle is real! The victories in Christ Jesus by the Holy Spirit are sweet and joyful. Many believers don't see themselves as they are in truth, and so don't appreciate what they have in Christ so they never scripturally obtain every spiritual blessing in the heavenly realms.

The Victorious Life in the Spirit

The believer who can fully understand Paul, both positionally and conditionally, understands that the believer's blessings and power are in the new man. In the new man there is no condemnation in Christ, because Christ was punished by death on a cross for us. Yet, through the old man, condemnation is all he produces. The victory of the new man is found when the believer starts to deal with the past sin, curses, and even generational issues. Every Holy Spirit-filled believer understands that the power of the fallen is in the choices of all generations just as the power of demonic spirits are in the words and deeds of all generations. These are facts I've learned in 22 years of demonic deliverance and 10 years of fallen angel judgments. Again, we are not condemned spiritually, but in the flesh, there are spiritual iniquities that condemn us. What is Paul's answer for us? The power of the life giving Holy Spirit has set us free from the law of sin and death. If we look closely, this is two-fold! Spiritually, we have become alive in Christ and are set free from eternal death immediately. But to be set free from the law is different. Positionally, we are set free from the law and, conditionally, we are being set free from the law. Freedom from the law is a sanctification process, but the power of sanctification is found in identification. Identification is the legal side of our redemption. It unveils to us what God did in Christ for us, from the time Jesus went to the cross, until He sat down on the right hand of the Father. Paul says in Galatians, "I have been crucified WITH CHRIST," we died WITH Christ, and that we were buried WITH Christ. This is one of the great keys that unlocks the teaching of the old man and new man. Paul says that Christ became one with us in sin, that we might become one WITH Jesus in righteousness. In Ephesians 2:6, "And raised us up WITH him, and made us to sit WITH him in the heavenly places, in Christ Jesus." This and other scriptures reveal our legal side, and it is in our legal side that we defeat the fallen angels. It is in our sanctification side that we are set free from demonic spirits. Colossians 2:13, "And you, being dead through your trespasses and the uncircumcision of your flesh, you I say, did he make alive together WITH Him." Romans 6:5, "for if we have become united WITH him in the likeness of his death, we shall be also in the likeness of his resurrection."

In Romans 8:3,4, it says, God sent His own Son in a human body like ours, except that ours are sinful, and destroyed sin's control and power over us by giving Himself as a sacrifice for our sins. It is through this sanctification process that we now can obey God's law if we follow after the Holy Spirit and no longer obey the old evil nature within us.

Those who choose to let themselves be controlled by their old man, that lower nature, live only to please that satanic principle. But following after the Holy Spirit, we find ourselves doing those things that please God, and it brings us life and peace. Yet, the old man within us is against God and it will never obey God's laws and those things that bring blessing. That is why those who are still under the control of their old man, Satan's will, are bent on following their old man with its evil desires, can never please God. I am writing in this manner to bring to light what is hidden in darkness. We understand this in some form theologically, but most are clueless spiritually. The key to understanding the New Testament is understanding theologically and supernaturally the old man and new man.

However, we are not like that if we have been filled with the Holy Spirit. We don't follow after the old man, because we are controlled by the new man, which is the power of the life in Christ through the Holy Spirit. Even though Christ dwells in our spirit man, the new man, our bodies that house the old man will die because of sin, the satanic principle. Here is a powerful principle that needs some thought: if the Spirit of God who raised up Jesus dwell in the new man, the Holy Spirit will make our dying bodies live again after we die. Spiritually, if the Holy Spirit has been granted through the work of Christ to resurrect our human bodies, then He today has a legal right to heal and deliver these dying bodies.

The new man has no obligations whatsoever to the old man to do what the old man desires. The sinful desires when acted upon bring demonization and sickness. Paul says that if we keep on following the old man we perish now and possibly for eternity. But through the new man and the power of the Holy Spirit we crush the old man and the satanic principle (nature of the devil) we will live and be blessed. Why? Because through the new man who is empowered by the Holy Spirit, we are led and we enter into sonship in Christ. This is why we are to grow up into our salvation or grow up into the new man, who is the image of Christ's likeness.

The new man behaves like God's children, one who is experiencing their adoption and the family, calling God Father! God's Holy Spirit speaks to us deep within our new man, the heart, and tells us what we really are, thereby we are empowered again to live for God through the Christ-life. This means restoring God's image and likeness in the creation. Since we are now His children through the new man, we will both in the now and future share in God's treasures, because all God gave to His Son Jesus, in Christ, we were and are to experience that treasure. The true treasure through the new man is the fullness of Christ Jesus. This is the reason God saved mankind, that through Jesus mankind would restore God's image, likeness, and authority in the earth. This is what it means to share in His glory, coming into the fullness of the new man, which is the image and likeness of Christ Jesus.

Even if we have to suffer in this tent, the old man, putting off the old creation, both spiritually and conditionally. Living from the new man and coming into the fullness of the new man cannot compare to the glory God is giving and will give in the new man. We should realize all creation is waiting patiently and hopefully for that future day. But the creation is responding today to the glory of the new man as he progresses and is molded into the image of Christ. As Christ is formed in us, sickness has less and less effect, just as sin does. This is a true reality! As the body of Christ becomes a bunch of children (new man), those children become one new man corporately. The creation, notice the word creation, visible and invisible which Paul refers to, waits with expectation for the sons of God to be revealed. I do understand the future intent here, but the kingdom and sonship is now, so the creation undergoes measures of transformation as the sons exercise God's authority and power through His likeness and image. This is how the fallen angels are taken out. As principalities (regions of land), principalities in the second heaven are dethroned. As Jesus commanded the creation, the creation is ready to respond to the believer or believers who are transformed into the Christ likeness, the new man!

The whole creation is suffering or groaning in sin's agony! We Christians have the Holy Spirit within us as we foretaste the futures glory by releasing that glory today! Because we are tasting the power and authority in our new man, we burn with passion and anxiously wait for that day when God will give us our full rights as His children, including the new bodies governed by the new nature as He promised us. These new bodies that we will have in the future is promised never to be sick again or die because of sin. We all know this to be true, so the Holy Spirit through the new man is working on us so that we can have many measures of that fulfillment. We are experiencing our salvation in measures today!

In our new man by faith, the Holy Spirit helps us with our daily problems and weakness knowing that all things are working out for the good as we pursue growth in the new man. This is God's purpose, the believer and the corporate believers coming into the power of sonship, which is the new man.

I will close this book with one last point that is of great importance! As we might notice, I closed the last chapter with this same thought. The purpose of God in bringing forth many children is to bring a collective body of believers as one new man as stated in Ephesians 2:14-15.

For He Himself is our peace, who made both groups into one and broke down the barrier of the dividing wall, by abolishing in His flesh the enmity, which is the Law of commandments contained in ordinances, so that in Himself He might make the two into one new man, thus establishing peace, Ephesians 2:14-15 NASB

God's overall purpose for the new man is a body of believers operating as one new man. This cannot happen unless the Church turns back to the Holy Spirit. God's design is for the new man to operate through a corporative body, the Church, to bring forth His likeness and authority. Notice Ephesians 4:16, "from whom the whole body, being fitted and held together by what every joint supplies, according to the proper working of each individual part, causes the growth of the body for the building up of itself in love." We are to be one complete corporate body expressing one new corporate man. This new man is to reenact Christ's earthly ministry and in so doing fulfills God's two purposes, revealing God to the world and exercises God's authority in Christ Jesus. By God's design, from the new man God's authority and power will bring a harvest of daunting proportions through the preaching of the gospel with signs and wonders. As the collective new man goes forward, the original purpose from the garden of Eden is reinstated. Be fruitful in Christ and multiply as disciples and fill the earth by subduing it in God's likeness and authority!

"Behold, I (Jesus) am coming quickly, and My reward is with Me, to give to each one according to the merit of his deeds (earthly works, faithfulness). I am the Alpha and the Omega, the First and the Last, the Beginning and the End [the Eternal One]." Blessed (happy, prosperous, to be admired) are those who wash their robes [in the blood of Christ by believing and trusting in Him—the righteous who do His commandments], so that they may have the right to the tree of life, and may enter by the gates into the city. Revelation 22:12-14

Resources:

Amplified Bible (AMP)
Copyright © 2015 by The Lockman Foundation, La Habra, CA 90631
The Holy Bible, New King James Version Copyright © 1982 by Thomas Nelson, Inc.
Nelson, Thomas. Holy Bible, New King James Version (NKJV) . Thomas Nelson. Kindle Edition.

New American Standard Bible-NASB 1995 (Includes Translators' Notes)
Copyright © 1960, 1962, 1963, 1968, 1971, 1972, 1973, 1975, 1977, 1995 by The Lockman Foundation
A Corporation Not for Profit, La Habra, California
All Rights Reserved

The Lockman Foundation. New American Standard Bible-NASB 1995 (Includes Translators' Notes) (Kindle Locations 1410-1412). The Lockman Foundation. Kindle Edition.

Logos Bible Software 7 - Copyright 1992-2018 Faithlife/Logos Bible Software.
© 1998 by InterVarsity Christian Fellowship/ USA ® All rights reserved. No part of this publication may be reproduced, stored in a retrieval system or transmitted in any form or by any means, electronic, mechanical, photocopying, recording or otherwise, without the prior permission of InterVarsity Press.
Leland Ryken, James C. Wilhoit, Tremper Longman III. Dictionary of Biblical Imagery (p. 1058). InterVarsity Press. Kindle Edition.

Derek Prince MP3 - The Old Self And New Self

Made in the USA
Columbia, SC
19 June 2019